About the Author

Born in England in 1942, now living in the dales he so passionately and eloquently describes in poetic form, David Pitman started writing poetry ten years ago. The variety of subjects which are covered in this anthology reflects his many interests in the world about us and his career in science. He claims his love for poetry was inspired by enjoying well-known classical rhyming poetry when he was very young. His rhyming verse is written in a style which will appeal to all ages with its humour, originality and fascination with the topics covered. The author would be pleased if it encouraged others to take an interest in the same topics and delighted if it inspired youngsters of today to take an interest in poetry.

About the Illustrator

Graphic artist, illustrator, miniaturist, photographer and founder of several poetry/writing groups in the N.W. area of England, Victoria Copeland has been drawing and painting since early childhood. In her youth, art college studies provided the discipline needed to further a natural creative talent. This talent, together with her previous experience in illustrating poetry anthologies, enabled her to interpret and create artwork to complement the range of subjects covered in the author's poetry, thereby providing a combination of verse and images to be enjoyed by readers of all ages.

POETRY FOR THE YOUNG AT HEART

David Pitman

Published in 2014 by the author

Text Copyright © David Pitman 2014
Illustrations © Victoria Copeland 2014

ISBN 978-1-78132-182-9

British Library Cataloguing in Publication Data
A CIP catalogue record for this book is available from the British Library

Printed by Berforts on responsibly sourced paper

Contents

Part 1

Hill, Dale and Woodland

Ingleborough

Oh Ingleborough, we know your shape,
We come to gaze, we come to gape,
In winter such a splendid sight
As snowstorms leave you clothed in white,
We wonder as we climb and walk,
What you could say if you could talk,
The Norber boulders – do they hide
The riddle of an ice age ride?
Did Simon fall, on Simon Fell?
Does Gaping Gill go down to hell?

Oh Ingleborough, through brook and burn,
As sediment you must return,
When slowly and remorselessly
Your scree is carried to the sea.
And when you're gone, what will be there?
And who will see and who will care?
Will nature's forces act once more
To shear and shape the old sea floor?
And will another ice age reign
To carve that well known brow again?

Oh Ingleborough, what did they see
When Stone Age humans looked on thee?
That noted shape, so well defined,
A landmark in an ancient mind.
And under what exotic skies
The story of your past life lies?
Oh Ingleborough, what could we glean
Of all the ages you have seen?
What timeless tales you could have told,
So silent, like the Sphinx of old.

The Enchanted Fell

In spring one day, I ventured forth
Along the fell to stroll,
I read the map and set off north,
The summit was my goal.

I scrambled up the steep fell side
Along a grassy track,
Here purple heads of orchids hide,
Their leaves with spots of black.

I wandered through a woody glade,
A haven for wild deer,
So here they linger in the shade,
I saw their tracks, quite clear.

A willow warbler caught my ear
From high up in a tree,
His song so sweet and full of cheer
Brought happiness to me.

The woodland violet there I found,
So delicate and shy,
Nearby I heard a faint soft sound,
Was that a fairy's sigh?

A whiff of scent, a fragrant tease,
Some bluebells on my right,
Their bells will tinkle in the breeze,
When fairies are in flight.

Wood sorrel grew there next to mould,
Each tiny bell in white,
Their leaves like clover with a fold,
Where pixies hold them tight.

I came upon a limestone edge,
To clamber up – a test,
Quite soon I sat down on a ledge,
A secret place to rest.

I found the summit point a last,
My eyes took in the view,
The Pennine hills, a range so vast,
Against a sky so blue.

I wandered back along the hill,
My mind full of delight,
On this spring day I've had my fill,
Of fragrance, sound and sight.

This charming hill has cast its spell,
A place for which I yearn,
Here magic and enchantment dwell,
One day I shall return.

Nature's Charms

How sweetly nature treats the eye,
Brings delight with a damsel fly,
Warms our hearts, so we wish to dwell,
Weaves its charms with an orchid's spell.

How sweetly nature's sirens call,
A perky wren that cheers us all,
The skylark singing on the wing,
A bittern's boom that broadcasts spring,

How sweetly nature lures us back,
Through bluebell woods along a track,
Dense fragrance hanging under trees
Delights the senses, in the breeze.

How sweetly nature spins its web,
While all the seasons flow and ebb,
How pleasing nature seems to man,
Enjoy it all, while you still can.

The Dream

On Scottish hills one summer's day,
Through fields and moors I made my way,
A warm, bright sun upon my back,
I followed up a winding track.

Then round a corner on my right,
A ruined croft came into sight,
I had not meant to linger there,
But something made me stop and stare.

No roof, no windows, no front door,
The walls were crumbling to the floor,
Amidst the ruins a fallen beam,
The remnants of a long lost dream.

I wondered how the dream did start,
Perhaps a union of the heart,
A horse and carriage brought them here,
A man and wife, a dream so clear.

On warm spring days, he digs the land,
The man, hard working, strong and tanned,
The woman singing, soft but fine,
Whilst hanging washing on the line.

Perhaps for life their dream did last,
Now only ruins, their lives long passed,
I thought about the love they had,
Then walked away, my heart quite sad.

And as I walked I could just hear,
A woman singing, soft but clear,
A sound that lingered in the air,
The dream still lived, I heard it there.

Portland Stone

One day I walked just for a thrill,
Along the cliffs to Portland Bill,
Three miles of splendour in the sun,
A joyous walk for anyone.

Along the edge I made my way,
A deep blue sea set in the bay,
The Chesil Beach off to my right,
Ran curving west, till out of sight.

At Blacknor Point, I paused to see
A rough route down that tempted me,
Not thinking of the hard climb back,
I scrambled down the steep, loose track.

Down by the shoreline, there I found
Amongst the pebbles, large and round,
An ammonite beneath a stone,
A spiral gem from time unknown.

I stopped to rest there by the sea,
Enjoying all the scenery,
Small waves broke softly on the shore,
I stayed awhile and wished for more.

With Portland Bill as my next stop,
I climbed back up, right to the top,
Then walked the cliff edge, sheer and high,
With seagulls soaring in the sky.

Soon, further on, I came to pass
Fresh fragrant orchids in the grass,
Here once again the cliffs were steep,
The sea beneath looked dark and deep.

Then by the coastguard – hard to find,
A steep climb down, the secret kind,
Not seen at all when walking by,
But one can find it – should one try!

At Portland Bill, an awesome sight,
A tide race showing all its might,
The lighthouse standing, proud and high,
To warn the ships that pass on by.

I still recall that day quite well,
That walk on which my thoughts can dwell,
I'll not forget because I own
That fossil found beneath a stone.

On Whernside's Slopes

On Whernside's slopes, men now unknown,
With skill and pride once quarried stone,
The rock from which the millstones came,
Hence how this mountain got its name.

On Whernside's slopes a north wind blows,
A biting chill the dog-fox knows,
While grouse seek cover in the night,
The frost leaves dry stone walls in white.

On Whernside's slopes a cloud will stay,
And drizzle spoils the shepherd's day,
His dog won't care, it will not stop,
But run and run, right to the top.

On Whernside's slopes the curlew calls,
Soon after dawn until dusk falls,
A joyous bubbling song of spring
And all the blessings it will bring.

Nature's Moods

The summer dies and autumn's born,
September days are here,
The fields still hold their bales of corn,
Displaying summer's cheer,
The lazy sun retreats each day,
Too weakened now to want to stay,
So migrant birds fly on their way.

November's mood is damp and cold,
But still the robin sings,
This tiny bird so blithe and bold
Ignores cruel winter's stings,
Then dawn unfolds one day to show
A sprinkled layer of fresh white snow,
An icy warning life should know.

When January comes our way,
With dark clouds in the skies,
Then winter's gloom seems here to stay,
Its sun so slow to rise,
But soon the shoots of green show through
And snowdrops bloom for all to view,
A sign that spring will start anew.

Twistleton Fell

The sun shone down on Twistleton Fell,
As I climbed up on the moor,
Along a track I remembered well,
For I'd walked here once before.

The wind turned cold on Twistleton Fell,
When I reached an upright stone,
How long it had stood I couldn't tell,
Left there by a force unknown.

The clouds grew dark on Twistleton Fell,
There were raindrops in the air,
I knew it would mean a stormy spell,
But in truth I didn't care.

The rain came down on Twistleton Fell,
It was followed by strong hail,
I stood all alone in a wild white hell,
But my spirit didn't fail.

The sun shone down on Twistleton Fell
When the ground was glistening white,
I gazed all about in a blissful spell,
Absorbing a wondrous sight.

I walked on down from Twistleton Fell
Wishing I had time to stay,
I looked back around as a last farewell,
Then vowed to return some day.

On a March Afternoon

With winter still clinging and frost on the ground,
I followed a footpath I'd recently found,
The sun falling back from the sky, far too soon,
Gave welcoming warmth on a March afternoon.

The path led through limestone, surmounted with ease,
Where moss covered boulders lay in amongst trees,
There was dew in the sun but frost in the shade,
Melting quite fast in the footprints I'd made.

A huge old beech tree soon loomed into sight,
I gazed up in awe impressed with its height,
The past season's foliage, the densest here found,
Now lay as a carpet, spread out on the ground.

Two young roe deer danced off through the trees,
Warned in advance by my scent on the breeze,
Then further on down a sound to enthrall,
A stream running over a small waterfall.

I saw buds on the oak, the hawthorn, the birch,
There were buds to be found wherever I'd search,
Raising my hopes that spring would come soon,
Lifting my soul on a March afternoon.

Secrets Near Silverdale

There's Lots to see by Morecambe Bay,
Where orchids sprout green wings in May,
The headland Jenny Brown might grace,
Here lady's tresses fall in place.
Then Adam's mate would find it nice
To climb up high and look for spice,
And Woodwell is the place to see,
A finch beside a hawthorn tree.

Gait Barrows' walks are so much pleasure,
Rare butterflies and plants to treasure,
The Duke might show if days are fine
A pedigree of French red wine.
You'll find a primrose if you try
That catches every songbird's eye,
And by the limestone where it's shady,
Look for a slipper from a lady.

Trowbarrow shows in warm June weather
How fly and orchid come together,
To find the seabed, look up high
For relics of a time gone by.
On Beetham Fell – a walk that's good,
Through ground that underlays a wood,
Squeeze up small steps, it's very tight
And see a fairy – you just might!

In a Bluebell Wood

I once found a frog in a bluebell wood,
Hiding away as well as it could,
Patiently waiting to ambush the flies,
Watching the world with its sharp little eyes.

I lingered awhile in that sweet sea of blue,
Dappled with light where the sun shone through,
And the song of a thrush was the only sound,
As I listened entranced and gazed all around.

I envied that frog in its bluebell delight,
With a soft bed of moss to rest for the night,
Then bask in the sun where the orchids grow,
Near a small shallow pond that a frog should know.

Now life as a frog would not be bad,
If one had the things that this good frog had,
Consider the thought that it would be nice
To live as a frog – in a frog's paradise.

Part 2

The Wonder of the Universe

Starry Night

I walked out on a starry night,
A bright full moon on high,
The stars above, a wondrous sight
Like diamonds in the sky.

The night was cold, the air was still,
A frost was forming fast,
I started up a short, steep hill,
My breath in steam was cast.

The moon, that artist of the night,
Shone on the frosted grass,
Brushed everything in silver white
And coated it with glass.

Upon the crest I had to stay,
I looked around in awe,
The universe before me lay,
A gleaming visual tour.

I saw Orion standing high,
The Dog Star followed near,
Distinctive in the southern sky,
The hunter's shape, so clear.

Then from the east a shooting star,
A streak I barely saw,
A second came bright from afar,
I wished I could see more.

Perhaps I lingered long to stare,
I really could not say,
But part of me I left up there,
When I went on my way.

Life, the Universe and Me

A myriad of stars shine up in the sky,
Great numbers of suns with planets nearby,
Worlds like our own where life could survive,
Mountains and valleys where things are alive,
Sometimes I think that it cannot be so,
Sometimes I think that no one can know.

A billion bright galaxies out there in space,
And in each perhaps, lives an alien race,
Intelligent creatures with strange looking eyes,
And some must look up, at night to the skies,
Sometimes I think that it cannot be so
Sometimes I think I'm not meant to know.

One day out in space a bright nova shows,
From earth it just seems like a new star that glows,
A signal that tells us that life had to die,
And nothing survives to ask questions why,
Sometimes I think that it cannot be so,
Sometimes I think I'd rather not know.

Spacetime is expanding as far as can be,
Outside of this limit there's nothing to see,
Before it all started, nothing was there,
And when it's all over, no one will care.
Sometimes I think that it cannot be so,
Sometimes I think that I'll never know.

Nothing is Real

Nothing is real, are the words of the song,
All that we know is possibly wrong,
Nothing we see is quite what it seems,
We live in a universe stranger than dreams.

Nothing is certain the physicist said,
Schrodinger's cat could be living but dead,
Nothing we touch is really all there,
Atoms are nothing much more than thin air!

Nothing is written that can't be rubbed out,
Texts can have authors which experts will doubt.
Nothing you're told can be taken as read,
The voice that you hear may be just in your head.

Nothing is there when we get to our goal,
It's all just a mirage that hides in our soul,
Nothing is real, are the words of the song,
We know nothing else, so we all sing along.

A Shining Light

Albert Einstein, a genius true,
By birth he was a German Jew,
Not seen when young, as one to note,
"He needs to work," his teacher wrote.

In college days he showed no spark,
He ended up a patent clerk,
This gave him time to think things through,
His bright ideas were all quite new.

When light beams shine – what could it be?
He worked it out, what he could see,
Not just a wave – a cyclic beat,
But bits of light, each quite discrete.

Quite soon his thoughts began to pay,
The Nobel Prize, it came his way,
His new ideas defied convention,
Time became the fourth dimension,

He set new rules that time would heed
When motion reaches near light speed,
That clocks slow down for those in flight,
Nothing can change the speed of light.

He solved the long term mystery
How mass converts to energy,
The power that lies within the sun
Was understood by everyone.

But Einstein hadn't finished yet,
On gravity his mind was set,
All science followed Newton's Laws,
But Einstein found some fatal flaws.

Day and night though he was weary,
He worked on his General Theory,
Showed gravity was not a force,
But curves in space bent things off course.

Then proof was sought and tests were done,
The moon in line would hide the sun,
The sun's huge mass should bend the light,
And so it showed – Einstein was right!

In genius terms he rates the best,
A quantum step above the rest,
And fittingly described by some,
"A shining light, whose time had come".

The Expansive Universe

Consider the present, know of the past,
Think of the future – it won't always last.
First came the Big Bang, when all had begun,
From it came the matter – before there was none.

Nothing was denser or hotter to start,
The heat was much greater than stars at their heart.
In less than a second it grew lightning fast,
A whole solar system would know of its blast.

Then as it grew larger the temperature fell,
And crystals of matter condensed from the swell.
Electrons and protons when hot, won't unite,
But once they have cooled, then there will be light.

From this came the night sky, the stars every one,
From this came the planets, from this came the sun.
Though all is expanding, they move not at all,
But deep space between them extends to the call.

Outside of the boundaries is no place to be,
With limited senses there's nothing to see.
Now destiny beckons and all share that fate,
Look into the the future before it's too late.

Eventually matter will be drawn apart,
Then energy only remains at the heart.
Since the whole process produced energy,
A born again universe there might again be.

Looking Up

What is this universe I see?
The stars at night shine down on me,
A billion torches held on high,
I know not how, I know not why!

What is this universe I see?
Vast galaxies seem small to me,
From deep in space they glow with light,
Far back in time, till out of sight.

What is this universe I see?
When shooting stars streak over me,
They end with glory in the sky,
As one by one they flare and die.

What is this universe I see?
The moon caught by earth's gravity,
Is held to waltz around the sun,
An endless dance, till time is done.

What is this universe I see?
Its birth, its growth, its history,
Who has the wisdom to define
The purpose of such grand design?

Back to the Future

Get back into the future,
Look forward to the past,
Exist outside the present,
Your universe is vast.

This is the fifth dimension,
Where here is always there,
A cube can have no corners
And circles can be square.

Here, time has no real meaning
And clocks are cast aside,
There is no late or early
And logic is no guide.

Due north has no location
And east lies to the west,
Below is right above you,
Whoever would have guessed?

All routes will lead you nowhere,
Each landmark is a trap,
The goal posts keep on moving,
You're always off the map.

Get back to the future,
The past will soon arrive,
Don't linger in the present,
Get into overdrive!

Jewel of the Night

Jupiter, Jupiter, jewel of the night,
We see you above us and gaze with delight,
For billions of years glowing with pride,
You've circled the sun on your heavenly ride.

Jupiter, Jupiter, jewel of the night,
A beacon of brilliance and joy to our sight,
Dancing your way through a background of stars,
Bigger than Saturn and brighter than Mars.

Jupiter, Jupiter, jewel of the night,
Gleaming so brightly, a celestial sight,
Supreme by your size, divine by your name,
You shine in the dark to show off your fame.

Poetry of the Planets

The sun has nine planets and as we have found,
Four are just gaseous and five have hard ground,
The gas giants are largest and coldest they say,
But rock worlds are warm, here life has its day.

Near to the sun hides one shy little star,
Of all the planets the smallest by far,
Mercuric by name, for the speed of its flight,
It's as though it is trying to keep out of sight.

The goddess of love, a planet so bright,
The evening star that sets in the night,
Time is no problem, there is no rush here,
For a day on Venus lasts more than its year.

A blue and white gem, the Earth has no peer,
A planet of value for life is found here,
Not short of water with oceans deep blue,
A world that's alive with plenty to view.

No life on Mars, it's believed to be dead,
Just deserts here on this planet that's red,
On each of the poles the ice is so dry,
It melts into vapour, straight up in the sky.

The largest gas giant, Jupiter by name,
And seen on its surface, the red spot of fame,
With sixteen close moons and one quite a sight,
Europa has water – and life, it just might!

Saturn shines brightly, in far space it's found,
Its ring is a wonder, so perfectly round,
Just frozen gases, that's all, in this sphere,
And too cold by far for life to start here.

The father of giants, Uranus the great,
Bows down to the sun, its spin is not straight,
Like a ship on its side, it lies out of phase,
Struck by a large mass in earlier days.

Neptune the mystic, not seen by the eye,
The god of the sea stays submerged in the sky,
Its striking blue colour is veiled by five rings,
Eight moons in close orbit, to all which it clings.

Pluto is a puzzle so far out in space,
A small icy planet, it seems out of place,
Perhaps it is true, the answer's not clear,
It's just a large comet that ended up here.

Part 3

For Younger Readers

Flight

Does an ostrich ever sigh
And wish it still could fly?
Would it be a bit absurd
To point out that it's a bird?
And its wings, I think you'll find,
Are of the feathered kind.
If it ran at twice the rate,
With its wings held out dead straight,
It could take off with a prayer
And fly – well, who knows where?

Does a penguin ever wish
It could catch its fill of fish,
By swooping down from high
Like a missile from the sky?
Well, if it had the drive
Having seen a gannet dive,
Then when it wants to feed,
It could always match that speed,
Down an iceberg it would ski
To plunge into the sea.

Could an elephant ever fly?
Or would it even try?
It could grow much larger ears,
Then advised by engineers,
If it flapped them really hard,
It might rise up a yard.
If it needed height, you see,
It could leap out of a tree!
Or perhaps a better bet,
It should board a Jumbo Jet.

Night Time

When children lie in bed and rest,
When birds sleep soundly in the nest,
When the fieldmouse hits the hay,
Then the stars come out to play.

When the bat flies in the sky,
When the hawkmoth flutters by,
When flowers close up for the day,
Then the stars come out to play.

When fairies dance round in a ring,
When you hear the nightjar sing,
When you see the sun's last ray,
Then the stars come out to play.

When rabbits in their burrows hide,
When pixies on the dormouse ride,
When the squirrel's in his dray,
Then the stars come out to play.

When the fox creeps from its den,
When the clock shows half past ten,
When the barn owl seeks its prey,
Then the stars come out to play.

When front doors are bolted tight,
When the moon shines in the night,
When a ghost slips on its way,
Then the stars come out to play.

Where Fairies Dance

Come follow me friend, to a woodland glade,
Walk under oak trees, cool in the shade,
Linger and listen to the rustle of leaves
As through the woods the wind softly weaves,
See how the sunbeams shine to the ground,
Highlighting bluebells spread all around,
Surely a place where pixies will prance,
Surely a place where fairies will dance.

Come follow me friend, when the sun burns low,
We'll walk along tracks where hobgoblins go,
Past where the barn owl perches on high,
Nothing that moves is missed by his eye,
Down by a stream there's a place that I know,
There you will find that the daffodils grow,
Surely a place where pixies will prance,
Surely a place where fairies will dance.

Boyhood Memories

I remember my first holiday,
The days spent by the sea,
The noise of gulls around the bay,
The sounds come back to me.

I recall picnics on the sands,
The family gathered there,
We'd brush the loose sand from our hands,
For food prepared with care.

I think of swimming by the shore,
The waves that chased me in,
The salty water felt so pure,
So cool against the skin.

I looked for shells in hidden coves,
I searched them in the sun,
In rocky pools and seaweed groves,
To find them – so much fun!

I yearn for days I can recall,
When fishing till last light,
The hours spent on the harbour wall,
Just waiting for a bite.

I remember days spent by the sea,
A young boy in the sun,
Those memories mean so much to me,
I treasure every one.

On Holiday at Cleveleys

We picnicked down upon the sand,
The week we spent at Cleveleys,
And in the sun we got quite tanned,
On holiday at Cleveleys.

Along the beach we splashed and swam,
The week we spent at Cleveleys,
Then off we went to catch a tram,
On holiday at Cleveleys.

We rode the tram to Fleetwood pier,
The week we spent at Cleveleys,
Then we eat fish and chips quite near,
On holiday at Cleveleys.

We spent some time at Blackpool, too
The week we spent at Cleveleys,
We saw the lions at Blackpool zoo,
On holiday at Cleveleys.

We've had some fun, we like it here,
The week we spent at Cleveleys,
We'd like to come another year,
On holiday at Cleveleys.

Does an Octopus Wish?

Does an octopus wish
It could swim like a fish
And glide through the oceans all day?
It could cling to the tail
Of a passing blue whale,
Provided there's no fare to pay.

Does an octopus dance
When it gets half a chance
With an octopus friend from next door?
They can shake, swing and sway,
In an eight-legged way,
Until they end up on the shore.

Does an octopus like
To go on a long hike,
Does it stroll on the seabed with ease?
When its boots are worn out,
In the shop, it will shout,
"Four pairs of these, if you please!"

Does an octopus eat
With its hands or its feet,
Does it handle a spoon like a dunce?
Will it drink all the wine,
Does it greedily dine,
And eat up eight courses at once.

Does an octopus hide
When a shark lurks outside,
Does it tremble and shake in its cave?
When the shark's out of sight,
Will it come out to fight,
And pretend that it's really quite brave?

Does an octopus laugh
While it's having a bath
When its mate gives its back a good scrub.
Does it giggle and shout,
Will it wriggle about,
Until they both fall out of the tub.

Does an octopus pray
At the end of the day
With its tentacles touching in pairs?
It could open its eyes,
Then look up to the skies
And hope to see God, if it dares.

Does an octopus scream
When it has a bad dream
Does it leap out of bed in a fright?
Can it hold back its tears,
Will it shrug off its fears
And sleep like a kipper all night?

Remember

Do not forget advice you've had,
From teachers, mentors, mum and dad,
Remember what your grandpa said,
Keep all that knowledge in your head.

Remember, brush your teeth at night
To keep them all a healthy sight,
Be smartly dressed when you've left school,
Your boss at work will think it's cool.

Remember too, down on the street,
Don't always trust grown-ups you meet,
No walking home alone, at night,
Be sure you have a friend in sight.

Remember, phone when you're away,
I want to hear what you will say,
Do not forget my birthday, ever
To fail on that would not be clever.

Don't be put off by family strife,
Stay with your partner all your life,
Remember, you'll have children too,
Advise them well, as I did you.

Remember all that I have said,
Now you're tucked up and snug in bed,
All sound advice and wisely told
To you, young girl, just three days old!

Freddie and Joe

Two men went cycling one fine day,
Freddie and Joe by name,
Touring the Chiltern Hills in May,
They'd often done the same.

For cycling it was hot that day,
But both kept up the pace,
Since neither wanted to give way,
The tour became a race.

They reached the hill back into Tring,
And Joe went speeding down,
To Freddie this meant just one thing,
A race back into town.

They both sped down to save their pride,
But bad luck came that day,
A lorry came out from one side,
And got in both men's way.

It was the speed that sealed their fate,
Their brakes just could not cope,
So Joe shot through an open gate,
And Freddie gave up hope.

Poor Freddie ended bruised and sore,
His handlebars were bent,
While Joe fell on a bale of straw,
His luck was heaven sent!

A lesson for both men that day,
That should be known to all,
Remember when you hear folk say,
"Pride comes before a fall!"

The Nile Crocodile

Swimming slowly up the Nile,
A fish came by a crocodile,
Staggered by its shape and size,
The fish could not believe its eyes,
It gaped and gazed without a care,
And fish should know – it's rude to stare!
But it kept thinking more and more,
This reptile was a dinosaur.

The fish kept swimming to and fro,
When wiser fish might choose to go,
Then cunningly, the crocodile
Displayed a toothy, kindly smile.
Which pleased the fish, it moved close in
To view this reptile with a grin,
How could a wide good natured smile
Belong on any bad reptile?

It would be sad to have to say,
Our friendly fish was lunch that day,
But nature helped our fishy friend
And saved it from a tragic end,
The fish was striped with bright red lines,
Which warned of venom in its spines,
The croc had tried this dish before
And wasn't keen to sample more.

It is with joy we can assert,
Our friendly fish escaped unhurt,
Still able now to swim about,
While one cross reptile went without,
To end this story, one could read
A message, which all fish should heed,
"Never, never, trust a smile,
Especially on a crocodile!"

Devilish

Why the devil does the devil
Do the things that devils do?
How the devil does he do it?
I could tell you if I knew.

If you're feeling like a devil
And have demons in your head,
Go and ring the devil's doorbell,
When he's fast asleep in bed.

If you bumped into the devil,
What the devil could you do?
You should smile just like a devil,
And say, "sorry – after you!"

If a demon is a devil
And an imp is like a sprite,
What the devil was that creeping
Round my bedroom overnight?

.

Part 4

Life, Present and Past

.

Lucy

In Africa they made a find,
An ancient relic of our kind,
The fossil bones reveal, they say,
An ape which walked the human way,

They found her footsteps set rock hard
Within a landscape baked and scarred,
Three million years back in the past,
The footprints dried, her steps were cast.

A life so hard, austere and bleak,
Not for the feeble or the meek,
Whilst all around great creatures call,
Just three foot high, she still walked tall.

With all the perils in her life,
She was a mother through the strife,
Her children grew, a family band,
Our ancestors who roamed the land.

Now words we write can bring to mind
The debt we owe her ancient kind,
For all to see, her footsteps stand,
A monument set in the land.

Coelacanth

Christmas, nineteen thirty eight,
A time they won't forget,
The final trawl was running late,
The fish was in the net.
They took it to the local dock,
There on the quay it lay,
A fish which wound back every clock,
Forgotten till that day.

An armoured fish with limblike fins?
There wasn't one around!
A look back through life's origins,
Some fossils had been found.
An ancient fish which didn't last,
A theory that seemed right,
But then this relic from the past,
Alive and full of fight.

Seventy million years had passed,
As back through time we gaze,
When fish like this were living last,
In those Cretaceous days.
The experts had a change of mind,
A fossil found alive!
A life they thought was left behind,
Had managed to survive.

Archaeopteryx

In ages past – that time forgot,
When Mesozoic days were hot,
Strange creatures flew from cliffs on high,
Their silhouettes framed in the sky,
Forms fully fledged, matured from chicks,
The feathered Archaeopteryx.

Now Darwin, Huxley – men of fame,
They knew this creature well, by name,
For nature showed, impressed in stone,
Its ancient structure, bone by bone,
This fossil found in limestone bricks,
The feathered Archaeopteryx.

Some experts claimed it was a bird,
Equipped with teeth – it seemed absurd!
But others said – a Pterosaur,
A flying reptile, not much more,
It keeps them guessing with its tricks,
The feathered Archaeopteryx.

Darwin

Charles Robert Darwin was the man,
Who made us think how life began,
Primeval soups and ancient gruels,
Organic cells in small warm pools.

The Church's teaching of the day
Showed God's creation was the way,
So fossils found down in the mud
Were just left over from the flood.

But Darwin saw each fossil cast
As just an echo of the past,
He saw features in the pieces
Bringing order to the species.

What Darwin saw was not a plan
Imposed by God on life and man,
Darwin had his own solution,
We call his theory evolution.

Using natural selection
Changed the way of life's direction,
It was a challenge to all life
To forge a way through storm and strife.

Then finally a showdown came
When Darwin publicised his claim,
Church and science met face to face,
The Oxford Union was the place.

The Bishop, Wilberforce by name,
Spoke up to prove the church's claim,
That man was placed by God on earth,
Not just an animal by birth.

Now Wilberforce was at his best,
He challenged rivals, half in jest,
"If from an ape you came," he cried,
"Was it on your mother's side?"

But science had a card to play,
For T.H. Huxley came that day,
As Darwin's bulldog he was known,
He chewed all critics to the bone.

When Huxley joined in this debate,
His eloquence changed Darwin's fate,
Hence evolution won the day
And Wilberforce went home to pray.

So chimpanzees and humans too,
And all the apes seen at the zoo,
As distant cousins can be cast,
With ancestors shared in the past.

Now Darwin's views are taught in schools,
All life evolved in ancient pools,
And man is not a special case,
Just one more runner in life's race.

Ode to a Mosquito

Anopheles,
Anopheles,
I hear your singing flight,
Stay off me, please,
Stay off me, please,
Don't pester me tonight.
You'd love to land
And make your mark,
Then leave me scratching
In the dark,
You've had your fun,
You came to tease,
It's time to go,
Now leave me, please!

Anopheles,
Anopheles,
I fear your tiny bite!
Get off me, please,
Get off me, please,
I cannot sleep for fright.
Your vampire way
Has pierced my skin
And now my hand
Will end your sin,
That's quite enough,
You had your chance,
Just one quick slap,
That's your last dance!

The Selfish Gene

Now listen to me, man machine!
Conveyor of the selfish gene,
You're just another phenotype,
Disguised in wishful human hype.

This knowledge roused you, wide-awake,
A bitter pill you've had to take,
Your actions ruled by coded genes,
To help them spread by selfish means.

Through branches in your family tree,
Each gene defines your pedigree,
You hold the torch then pass it on,
The flame still burns when you are gone.

The good die young, the genes don't care,
The bad live on – it isn't fair!
Your role in life – it's not that great,
Just helping genes perpetuate.

But genes gave you the means to think,
To write things down with pen and ink,
So thoughts survive for eons long,
Through book and story, verse and song.

With means to think, you have the choice
To disregard the selfish voice,
So go the way you know you should
And act as though your genes are good!

Starfish

Beneath the waves where the mermaid sighs,
On the sea floor where the flounder lies,
In the dark cold depths where lobsters tread,
A starfish sleeps on a sandy bed.

Just off the shore of a pebbly cove,
Along the reef in a coral grove,
Under a ledge where the eel-grass sways,
A starfish hides in a rocky maze.

At the end of a quay where seabirds call,
In deep water by the harbour wall,
As the fishing boats pass overhead,
A starfish feeds on a mussel bed.

On a treacherous reef a mile offshore,
Where a lighthouse shines and breakers roar,
In a sheltered pool throughout the night,
A starfish shows in the passing light.

Five fathoms down near a deep sandbar,
Lies the rotting hulk of the Eastern Star,
Near rusting rails on an ancient deck,
A starfish clings to the listing wreck.

Washed in by the waves, on the shore cast,
At a sandy beach, when life has passed,
A starfish lies quite still, by the sea,
Where it's often found by you and me.

The Naughty Nautilus

Here's to the Pearly Nautilus,
Its image almost infamous,
In ocean depths down out of sight,
It sleeps all day and eats all night,
Its nature nearly gluttonous,
So naughty is the Nautilus.

Here's to the Pearly Nautilus,
Its tentacles quite numerous,
Poor shrimps and prawns, they get no sleep
While this night hunter haunts the deep,
Its pastimes plainly barbarous,
So naughty is the Nautilus.

Here's to the Pearly Nautilus,
Its motives mainly villainous,
A throwback to the ammonites
With no real sense of other's rights,
Its conduct clearly scandalous,
So naughty is the Nautilus.

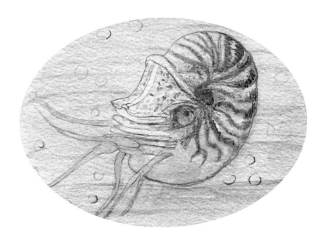

Predator

Like a ghost, silently,
In the depths, hard to see,
On the move, gliding free,
A great white shark makes its way,
Cruising on, round the bay.

On a board, well offshore,
Catching waves, breakers roar,
Out for kicks, wanting more,
The surfer waits in the tide,
Won't be long, one more ride.

Splashing arms, kicking feet,
Draws the shark, it must eat,
Senses flesh, glimpses meat,
The shark moves in, teeth show white,
Jaws converge, one big bite.

Filled with fear, shocked and jarred,
Makes for shore, swimming hard,
Getting back, yard by yard,
The board is lost, he won't mind,
Safe on shore, fate was kind.

Surfboard hit, missed its prey,
Hungry shark swims away,
Hunting still, round the bay,
The shark is young, in its prime,
Gaining skills, for next time.

Into the Unknown *(A Tribute to William Beebe)*

Climb into a sphere, its hull made of steel,
The hatch is screwed down to make a good seal,
Then into the sea to float for a while,
Before you will sink two thirds of a mile,
Into the deep blue, into the unknown,
Down to the depths, to the twilight zone,
Leaving behind a bright sunny day,
Blue sky and clouds now so far away,
Then as you descend the temperature falls,
Soon moisture collects, condensing on walls,
One tiny porthole through which you can peer
And see any life, which might just come near,
The beam of your light will not travel far,
Not really enough to see where you are,
At three thousand feet, you reach the seabed,
Then stay for a while and hang from a thread,
Before you return to that surface so clear,
To the sun and the sky, that now seem so dear.

Homo Erectus

One million years before man's birth,
Another walked upon this earth,
Part ape, part human, who can tell,
But standing tall, surviving well.

Compared to man, a modest brain,
It wasn't king of its domain,
But watchful, wily, wide-awake,
A streetwise biped on the make.

Near riverbanks and lakesides too,
The biped stayed, its numbers grew,
It found its food in this landscape,
An Eden for a manlike ape.

But often change is nature's way,
And polar ice caps came to stay,
In Africa the forests dried,
And deserts stretched on every side.

Along the coast the biped thrived,
When food was short then on it strived,
To forests new and creatures strange,
The biped coped with every change.

An ice age came, an ice age went,
Such frequent change left species spent,
But nature's mood as often can,
Shaped destiny for this apeman.

In gaining skills to problem solve,
The biped needed to evolve,
In time it learned to fashion stone,
The tools it used, it made its own.

An age then passed, a baby cried,
A human mother by its side,
One race was run, one more began,
A signal of the age of man.

Today we learn that people think
This biped was the missing link,
Homo Erectus was the key
To Homo Sapiens, you and me.

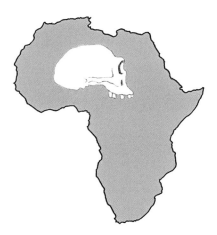

Part 5
Poetry for Fun

Grumpy Old Man

There's too much change in life today,
But what's improved – no one can say?
My memories now are just a haze,
But I prefer...the good old days!

It once was fun to own a car,
On roads today you don't get far!
You're on your way to view the sights,
But all you'll see is traffic lights!

There's nothing for you on TV,
Just this and that celebrity,
The films are always blood and guts,
Enough to drive a sane man nuts!

You can't find goods in any shops,
Your size or shape – they've not got stocks,
The internet is where you try,
Good services, we've kissed goodbye!

We live in this computer age,
You soon won't need the written page,
Now what you see is what you get,
I've seen it all – got nothing yet!

Those mobile phones are everywhere,
You hear their gossip – they don't care!
Some bury phones in graves, it's said,
So folk can phone back from the dead!

I moan about it, but who hears?
I'm sure it all will end in tears,
Don't try to change me, no one can,
I'm just an old and grumpy man!

The Mad Boffin's Teaparty

A group of boffins met one day,
For tea with cream and cakes,
They were so clever, people say
They never made mistakes.

They argued how the ocean tide
Moved round the planet's face,
It really should flow down the side
And fall off at the base.

First, Newton had his laws to state,
He said, "It seems to me,
If water had an apple's weight,
It would fall off a tree!"

Charles Darwin said, "I think I know,
It's natural selection,
For nature makes the water flow
And chooses its direction."

Einstein sketched it on the wall,
"You're all quite wrong," he said,
"The water doesn't move at all,
But spacetime moves instead!"

Then Freud got up to prove his worth,
He said, "I think you'll find
There is no water and no earth,
It is all in your mind!"

At Hubble's turn, he made no sound,
His thoughts were long and deep,
He kept them waiting till they found,
He'd fallen off to sleep!

Then Einstein finished eating cake,
"I've worked it out," he said,
"We could have made a big mistake
Or Freud is off his head!"

Poor Hubble woke and spilt his tea,
He could only splutter,
Then Newton laughed aloud in glee,
As Freud began to mutter.

A girl called Alice came to play,
She looked in by the door,
And when they had no more to say,
She spoke across the floor.

"The moon must make the tide go round,
It must exert a pull,
The higher tides are often found
Just when the moon is full!"

The boffins pondered in deep thought,
They had to all agree,
Their own ideas had come to nought,
Perhaps she'd stay for tea?

A lesson here for others, too,
Don't always think one way,
Stand back and take the wider view,
An open mind will pay.

Read All About It!

Tomorrow's new headlines, yesterday's news,
Political comment, editorial views,
Experts describing the latest health scares,
Read it at breakfast – who really cares?

Inflation is looming, bank rates will rise,
Fat cats get fatter, now there's a surprise!
Stock market prices, bulls, stags and bears,
Hedge funds need trimming – who really cares?

Celebrity gossip – who's in her bed?
He should know better, it's time they were wed,
Drugged to the eyeballs, she fell down the stairs,
He's dating her mother – who really cares?

Sport on the back page, a boxer is floored,
The footballer's story – with women he's scored!
Athletes miss dope tests then run like hares,
Boffins can't catch them – who really cares?

We read it at breakfast or while on a train,
We say it's all nonsense then buy it again,
We soak up the gossip, those tacky affairs,
Then quickly forget it – who really cares!

Horses for Courses

My filly's quite silly, I've heard people say,
That sorrel's immoral, it quarrels all day,
The donkey's a honky, not top of its class,
Don't be surprised if the mule is an ass.

That mustang's a must have, I've heard people say,
The blighter's a fighter, he'll grab all the hay,
Your racer's a chaser, it's not all that fast
Don't be surprised if it always comes last.

There's horses for courses, I've heard people say,
And ponies for cronies and phoneys who pay,
There's trotters for rotters, who mount up and go,
Don't be surprised if they ride Rotten Row.

Man's Best Friend

I'm considering a pet – I just have to choose,
A healthy young puppy I couldn't refuse,
A dog is a friend, protects you at night,
Keeps vandals away, gives burglars a fright.

"You should get a cat" – was someone's advice,
Then I'd be sure that my house has no mice,
It would sharpen its claws on the sofa, for sure
And leave muddy footprints inside the back door.

Some people like snakes – they just make me sadder,
I can't make a friend of an angry puff adder!
You can live in comfort, with things that you're fit for,
But I don't fancy life with a boa constrictor!

A budgie that talks would be a good friend,
I'd buy a posh cage, it's not much to spend,
Then I'd have room for a bird-eating spider,
But it would just end with the budgie inside her!

Now ladies like pets that are easy to feed,
They give them just scraps, food they don't need,
A pot-bellied pig suits them, I suppose,
With a husband at home – they've got one of those!

I've considered all aspects in search of my quest,
To think of the company that suits man the best,
Not just for Christmas but with you for life,
A husband's best friend, who else but...the wife!

Summertime Sometime

The summer's here, it's hard to know,
But if the rain stops out I'll go,
It's global warming experts say,
They know it brings the rain our way.

Last winter was the coldest yet,
All that snow I can't forget,
It's global warming they repeat,
I thought that warming meant more heat.

The wind gets stronger every year,
The forecasts, I can't bear to hear,
It's global warming people say,
The gale force winds are here to stay.

My latest gas bill I've not seen,
I know it's higher than it's been,
It's global warming they will say,
You use our fuel, you'll have to pay.

So when they claim that I've not paid,
I'll use the reason they have made,
It's global warming I will say,
The wind has blown your bills away!

Loads of Money!

I hope one day I'll make my stash,
I'll win a load of money,
I'll stuff my pockets full of cash
And fly to somewhere sunny.

I'd buy new things I wouldn't need
And boast that I could spare it,
They'll say I do it out of greed,
Well, they can grin and bear it!

A stately home would suit me fine,
I'd live it up and "lord it",
I'd have a cellar stocked with wine
Because I could afford it.

The land around would all be mine
From doorstep to horizon,
I'd plant the trees to grow in line,
A view to feast your eyes on.

And when one day I'll get God's call,
I'm sure he means to do it,
They'll bury me just where I fall,
And build a shrine next to it.

Screw it Up

I knew it would go wrong!
They get them from Hong Kong,
The instructions, if you please,
Have been printed in Chinese,
The handle doesn't fit,
Can't find the missing bit!
Today will end in sorrow,
Have another try, tomorrow.

I knew that I would break it,
They told me not to shake it,
I thought that I could glue it,
Now my trousers are stuck to it!
It doesn't stand up straight,
This always seems my fate,
I'll tell them I can't do it,
They'll laugh and say I blew it!

I knew that I would rue it,
They said, "You're welcome to it!"
It looked good on the stand,
When I bought it secondhand,
The battery has gone flat,
Well, I half expected that!
Can't say I never thought it,
I knew it when I bought it!

Fingers

There's ten of them of different size,
We use them when we're praying,
Their purpose is – said by the wise,
To stop our hands from fraying.

But apes and monkeys have them too,
A thumb and four strong fingers,
Just right to hold a branch, it's true,
That's why they're such good swingers.

We point one where you have to go,
To show in which direction,
We wave one when you have to know,
You're wrong, you need correction!

So useful too, they have no match,
They are such handy digits,
Without their help, we could not scratch,
We'd all be such bad fidgits.

Some people think it's quite benign
To use one when we beckon,
But those of us who use this sign,
You should not trust, I reckon!

So when the taxman comes to call
And for your cash, he lingers,
A sign that's known to one and all,
You give him just two fingers!

The Washing Machine

My door has been opened, they've put in some clothes,
They get them so grubby but how heaven knows,
I have fourteen programmes, they only use one,
They don't seem to know that the others will run.

I fill up with water then let in the soap,
The socks are quite smelly but I can still cope,
I heat up the contents and move round the clothes,
The drum is turned one way, then back round it goes.

The timer will tell me when washes are done,
I pump out the water then spin round for fun,
I'm ready to rinse now with water that's cold,
I'd rather stay warm but do as I'm told.

The fabric conditioner goes in at this time,
So all wool and cotton will be in their prime,
Then when I am ready I spin round like mad,
It makes me feel shaky which can be quite bad.

This batch has now finished, it seems to be fine,
They take out their clothing to hang on the line,
I've seen it quite dirty – the tales I could tell!
But now it's all spotless and that's just as well!

Part 6

Faith, Hope and Poetry

.

Messiah

Virgin's child, born as Messiah,
Son of Man but reached much higher,
King of Kings, crowned with ambition,
Came from God, sent on a mission.

"Follow me" – he gave men choices,
Spurning all the doubting voices,
"Leave the nets – it's men you fish for!"
Could he be the one they wish for?

Drew large crowds to hear him speaking,
He could be the one they're seeking!
Fed them full on loaves and fishes,
Would he satisfy their wishes?

Praised the poor, denounced the wealthy,
Healed the sick and left them healthy,
Blessed the child and shamed the sinners,
Told them how to be life's winners.

Dared to challenge those in power,
Captured at the midnight hour,
Treason was the charge intended,
Guilty was the way it ended.

Saint or saviour, sage or seer,
Lost his life but showed no fear,
Left his words for all to ponder,
Some still doubt and some still wonder.

Resurrection

Near a tomb outside a city
There is someone you should greet,
In a room inside that city
There's a man that you should meet,
You may wish to look more closely
Or just touch him to make sure,
Once you really get to know him
He's a man you can't ignore.

You might see him in the mountains
As you look into the sky,
On the shore when you are fishing,
He will sometimes catch your eye,
You could see him as a stranger
When you're walking on the road,
Where he goes, you'll want to follow
Down the way that he has showed.

Show Us!

Light from the fire in the heart of the sun,
Shine on the land when the day has begun,
Let every man feel the warmth from on high
Show us your flame, everyday till we die.

Waves from the sea breaking white on the shore,
Bring us the fish then we hunger no more,
Let every man fill his net from the surf,
Show how the sea gives a man what he's worth.

Rain from the clouds looming dark in the sky,
Quench all the ground for the crop to grow high,
Let every man take his share of the seeds,
Show how the earth gives a man what he needs.

Light from the gleam of the stars in the sky,
Shine on us all with such bliss to the eye,
Let every man be in awe at the sight,
Show us the way as you glow in the night.

Judgment Day

On Judgment Day, that final date,
The time that sinners dread,
When Ted stood there to hear his fate,
On rising from the dead.

"Your life of sin puts you to shame,"
St. Peter said out loud,
"And you have but yourself to blame,"
Whilst Ted stood there, head bowed.

"A few last words for every man,
A chance you don't deserve,
Defend yourself as best you can,
Your soul you could preserve."

So Ted stepped up to make his case,
No longer was he meek,
He stared St. Peter in the face,
And took a breath to speak.

"Your charge is weak, I'm not in fright,
I have no serious vice,
To scoff at me, you have no right,
For you, the cock crowed twice!"

St. Peter stepped back with a frown,
He clearly was put off,
St. John fell down and rent his gown,
St. Mark began to cough.

A mighty choir began to sing,
A light shone in the sky,
Then unseen bells began to ring
And God appeared on high.

But Ted was not to be denied
And he was plucky too,
"The Trinity at last!" he cried,
"Which one of three, are you?"

The face of God began to glow,
The eyes, they went quite red,
But Ted was not impressed below,
No words he left unsaid.

"Your name is honoured in the pew,
The Prince of Peace and more,
Yet bloodless times, we've had but few,
Why not the Prince of War?"

"We've suffered each and every year,
Don't dream we'd want you back,
If man could choose without a fear,
For sure you'd get the sack!"

"You've left the world in chaos now,
A stain upon your crown,
You ought to make your final bow,
It's time that you stepped down."

The face of God in anger broke,
Enough to make one dread,
Then vanished in a puff of smoke,
And Ted woke up in bed.

Ted's bold resolve, his dream so odd,
A guide to all mankind,
It can't be right to fear your God,
Stand up and speak your mind!

The Pagan Way

There is but one god, Moses said,
This message cannot be misread,
The first commandments carved in stone,
One god to worship, one alone.

In that form it's meant to stay,
Till one church council had its way,
For at Niceae, bishops mused,
Then left the Christian world confused.

The Trinity grew from this seed,
Proclaimed to all, a new church creed,
One god alone turned into three,
A Holy Ghost – what can that be?

Yet others haunt us from on high,
The devil tempts us till we die,
He's one more god, who's much the same,
Not one to praise but one to blame!

Still yet we have the saints to laud,
So numerous now and all adored,
These patron saints the church begats,
Just pagan heads in Christian hats.

Your patron saint or Holy Ghost,
You pray to whom you need the most,
Each holy figure waits on high,
Like old Greek gods up in the sky,

But if to all these gods we pray,
We worship in the pagan way,
If there's a god on which to call,
It must be one – or not at all!

In Search of God

In churches I looked everywhere,
In chapels I did seek,
I wished for God in pious prayer,
I tried hard every week.

I heard that God can speak to you,
He does not speak to me,
At every shrine I chanced to view,
No vision did I see.

I took my problems to the Dean,
Some questions I did ask,
The Holy Ghost he must have seen,
So help me in my task.

"Your quest will fail for sure, you see,
I know what you must do,
You must believe", the Dean did plea
"And God will come to you".

"But what when grief and sadness call?"
I questioned him anew,
"If Jesus died to save us all,
Why must we suffer too?"

"It's Satan's work", the Dean did say,
His cross upon his breast,
"For God is good and that's his way,
And Satan does the rest".

My troubled thoughts I share with you,
It's simple don't you see,
If I believe in Satan too,
Then Satan comes to me.

High Resolution

Where were you Lord, when Satan tempted Eve?
And Adam ate an apple, some believe,
They were no match for Satan's cunning ruse,
Why weren't you there to help them both refuse?

Where were you Lord, when Nero ruled with hate?
You left your trusting faithful to their fate,
Rome killed and tortured Christians every day,
How could you let them suffer in this way?

Where were you Lord, when faiths engaged in war?
Crusaders fought with Muslims and what for?
They met to slay, to slaughter and to maim,
But both sides claimed it was in your good name.

Where were you Lord, when heretics were burned?
To purify their souls or so they learned,
The victims could do nothing more than pray,
Your answer Lord, was just to turn away.

Where were you Lord, when men fought by the Somme?
And thousands died by bullet, shell and bomb,
Yet all believed that God was on their side,
You could have stopped it all, if you had tried.

Where were you Lord, when Hitler's plan worked well?
At Auschwitz, where the Jews were gassed in hell,
You saw them there and then you did no more,
Your chosen race, that you chose to ignore.

Where were you Lord, when sinners could all smirk?
When what we saw was just the devil's work,
Your New Year's resolution, let it be,
You could do so much better, it's our plea.

Life, They Say

Life, they say is just a test
To see if you can do your best
To play the cards that you've been dealt
And show your love is all heartfelt.

Life, they say is when you try
To look all evil in the eye,
And show no lack of strength and will,
For all your days be righteous still.

Life, they say can get you down,
But don't let others see you frown,
Just hear a lark sing in the sky,
And walk on smiling, head held high.

Life, they say is not so bad,
Just think of past good times you've had,
And when the days are wet and cold,
Your heart is warm, your thoughts are gold.

A Lion, a Lark and a Ladybird

A lion, a lark and a ladybird
In the shade of a coconut tree,
Talked of the the things that they had heard
On the shore of the Sapphire Sea.

"What," said the ladybird, "has God to do
When he stays in heaven all day?
What makes him different from me or you,
Or could he be a she, would you say?"

"A god" said the lion, "is known to be right,
He is never in the wrong,
But to be at the top, you have to fight,
So I think God must be strong."

"A god" said the lark, "can only sing
When he's soaring through the sky,
He looks down at us when he's on the wing,
For he's usually way up high!"

A man then approached from along the shore
By the side of the Sapphire Sea,
The ladybird asked him if he knew more,
To solve the quest of the three.

"Oh, yes!" said the man, "For I am the key
To the way God is displayed,
To understand God, you must look at me,
In his image, I am made!"

"Tush!" said the ladybird, "That's very odd,
Because it's plain for all to see,
If you are made in the image of God,
Then he must be a chimpanzee!"

"Pride," said the lark, "has dulled your mind,
No more of that, if you please!
If you could look back at your ancient kind,
They'd be swinging through the trees!"

"We've heard," said the lion, "of your pompous view,
You believe you share God's shape,
Now he's made a monkey out of you,
Because you're really just an ape!"

A lion, a lark and a ladybird,
In the shade of a coconut tree.
Made the boast of man seem quite absurd,
On the shore of the Sapphire Sea.

Thy Kingdom Come

The crowd calls out, the verdict stands,
A Roman Prefect cleans his hands,
A man is judged, his life must end,
No one will help, he has no friend.

One week before, he comes as King,
"Hosanna, Lord" the people sing,
This Lord who on a donkey rides
With palm leaves scattered on all sides.

This King who Judas then betrayed
And thirty silver coins was paid,
This Lord who all the people heard
And dwelt upon his every word.

The promise that he made so clear,
"The Son of Man soon will appear",
The prophecy, he could confirm,
"God's kingdom comes within your term".

Within their time no kingdom came,
No Son of Man for their acclaim,
Two thousand years, but still some wait,
This King, this Lord – forever late!

What If?

What if, when rich we gave away
A little to the poor each day?
What if, instead of being greedy,
We thought a moment of the needy?

What if, when on our soapbox proud,
We heard the voices in the crowd?
What if we spent some time each day
To listen to what people say?

What if – about to tell a lie,
We told the truth – it's worth a try!
What if, when heard, our word would hold
A pledge that's worth its weight in gold?

What if no God exists on high,
No judgment of us when we die?
What if in life, it is our plight
To be upstanding because it's right!

What if when young, you start a plan
To be as honest as you can?
What if you fail in this your mission,
You'll end up being a politician!

Part 7

Miscellaneous Poems

High Flier

The mayfly lives but one spring day
And in that time its life must pay,
To find a mate it must not tire,
For time is short for this high flier.

And you, my friend, are you the same?
Are you a part of some mad game?
You needn't work at such a pace,
Life's for living, it's not a race.

You're out on business once again,
With meals on board the high speed train,
No time to rest, you rising star,
The Joneses have a brand new car.

But when you work from eight till seven,
You haven't time to look for heaven,
So while you keep long office hours,
You'll never walk in fields of flowers.

One day for you is like the next,
Must phone that man, must send that text,
Must dash to catch that early plane,
Forget about that bad chest pain.

The mayfly's born without a gut,
It never eats, its mouth stays shut,
And you my friend, are you the same?
A mind that's closed – it's such a shame.

Now life has passed for you, high flier,
You've done so well, you've reached the spire,
But while you lived, you aimed so high,
You let the joys of life go by.

Wind of Change

In Africa, the time had come,
Colonial days, not good for some,
Now through the land a new wind blew,
The mood had changed, a dream came true.

In Zaire too, they felt the same,
A change of state, a change of name,
The colonies were falling fast,
The Third World could be free at last.

The Gold Coast went and Ghana came,
Nkrumah basked in all the fame,
But eight years on Nkrumah cried,
No money left, a dream had died.

The ghosts of leaders haunt the past,
Anwar Sadat – he didn't last!
Lumumba died, but by whose hand?
Mengistu ruled a barren land.

In sub-Sahara came the drought
Thousands starved, then war broke out,
Once more for freedom people died,
Once more their wishes were denied.

Rwanda saw the worst of man,
The Tutsis died, the Hutus ran,
A slaughter born of racial hate,
Provoked by bigots in that state.

Now fifty years have passed on by,
But still the people starve and die,
The cradle of mankind they say,
A place where man has lost his way.

Krakatoa *(1883)*

West of Java by Sumatra,
Near the narrow Straits of Sunda,
Almost on the earth's equator,
Stood the island Krakatoa.

Then one August sunny morning
Came a tremor, nature's warning,
Magma rising, steam compressing,
Pressure building, fissures stressing,
Soon the forces grew to breaking,
Overwhelming and earthshaking,
Then the final big eruption
Wreaked the havoc and destruction,
With a blast that rolled like thunder
All the mountain burst asunder,
Nature's mighty detonation
Only leaving devastation.

West of Java by Sumatra,
Near the narrow Straits of Sunda,
Magma proved to be the stronger,
Krakatoa is no longer.

Through a Glass Darkly

Through a glass darkly, a vision I see,
A shape in the mirror which cannot be me,
The eyes of a madman stare back at my face,
The hair is unruly, the clothes a disgrace.
I try not to look but it won't go away,
That looking-glass image, which haunts me each day.

Possessed by a devil, I roam down the street
And find only trouble with people I meet,
A conflict within me is taxing my soul,
Each day that goes by, I lose more control.
In bed I am restless, in dreams I must fight
The demons my conscience trawls up in the night.

The future lies empty, I won't fit in there,
The present confounds me, its people don't care,
The past is still with me, I think back each day,
Why did I decide to do things that way?
I'm caught in a time lag, an in between state,
Fighting delusions while awaiting my fate.

Philosophical Thoughts

When a rainbow paints its colours,
It is beauty to the eye,
If there's no one there to see it,
It's just raining in the sky!

When a tree falls in the forest
With an impact on the ground,
If there's no one there to hear it,
Then does it make a sound?

If a flower grows in the desert,
Where no one ever went,
If no creature's there to smell it
Then does it have a scent?

When you down a shot of whisky,
It feels strong and warm inside,
But if no one ever drank it
Would it still be good, untried?

There are answers to these problems
That a mastermind could see,
If you could ever solve them,
You'd be brainier than me!

Saturday with the Blues

You get it when you're very young,
A tribal hook on which you're hung,
There is no cure that's known to man,
You'll always be a football fan!

Just once a week you get the itch
To cheer and shout at fever pitch,
But fever can't be found in grass,
"It's in your mind, you silly ass!"

In rain or sunshine hail or snow,
Up to the stadium you must go
To stay and bear it with a grin,
When once again, your team won't win!

You watch your heroes every game
And every time it ends the same,
No matter how you cheer and roar,
They can't remember how to score.

It's not too much to ask – that's true!
For heaven's sake – one goal will do!
And when they lose, back home you'll go
To suffer hours of feeling low.

But if God wills, your team will play
At Wembley in the cup one day,
Your captain holds the trophy high,
It's just a dream – wake up and sigh!

No wonder that your heart feels sad,
Your brain tells you it's all quite mad,
But you know that next Saturday,
You will be there to watch them play.

A Shouting Man

I came upon a shouting man,
Bellowing rage as shouters can,
How strange it was that one could meet
A man so troubled on the street.

I stopped awhile that voice to hear,
Those words that rang out loud and clear,
Yet other folk just walked on by,
Pretending not to hear his cry.

His face unshaved, his hair unkempt,
His anger fuelled by their contempt,
He waved his arms to draw their eyes,
His words still bringing no replies.

On drink or drugs – who really cares
For this poor man who shouts and glares,
Some glanced his way to smirk and sneer,
Their scorn perhaps derived from fear.

There was no message in his sound,
He seemed to storm at all around,
I wondered how he slept at night,
His head consumed in mental fight.

Some said he should be locked away,
A padded cell is where he'd stay,
I felt some sadness and alarm,
He'd hurt no one, he'd done no harm!

Perhaps he's in that street today,
Still shouting loud as is his way,
I hope sometime he will find peace,
His anger quenched, his shouts will cease.

Reflections

Once in the Highlands in mid May,
I found an ideal base,
A fine old inn set by a bay,
Loch Leven was the place,

I saw a spot to park my car
And checked in at twilight,
Then joined some people at the bar,
We talked till late at night.

There was a portrait on the wall,
A haunting face, quite white,
Her eyes were dark, her mouth was small,
She was a troubled sight.

I asked someone if they knew more,
A local girl, he said,
The date was nineteen sixty four,
They found her floating, dead!

She walked from home one stormy night,
Went missing for three days,
Then on the loch an awful sight,
Her body on the waves.

I left the lounge bar in deep thought,
Wondering why she died,
They said that it was no one's fault,
A case of suicide.

The morning came quite dim and grey,
I walked down to the shore,
It was a quiet and lonely bay,
The air was cold and pure.

The loch was calm, the water clean,
There were no waves to see,
I looked down on the surface sheen,
The image was...just me!

Then suddenly the view was smeared,
My image was no more,
Instead a female face appeared,
A face I'd seen before.

Those haunting eyes, once more I saw,
That pale slim face again,
It was the same girl I am sure,
I swear I felt her pain.

Perhaps it's all just in my mind,
I have no answers yet,
Just memories of a ghostly kind,
A face I can't forget.

Climate Change Woes

We daren't heat our homes though winter bites cold,
We daren't fly on planes from what we've been told,
Then they will stop us from driving away,
We'll all sit at home and shiver all day.
If that's not enough there's soon to be seen
Increases in taxes, apparently green,
Our footprint of carbon is what it's about,
We need to reduce it or someone will shout.

It's all our own fault, we've been really bad,
We've caused global warming, we ought to be sad,
For carbon dioxide, the source of our woes
We're breathing it out, expelled through the nose,
Soon we'll be hit with a new tax, they say,
Whenever we breathe – we'll all have to pay!

Appledore

I left her down in Appledore,
The sky was blue that warm spring day,
I said goodbye, then said no more,
She claimed her love had died away.

I walked past cherry trees in flower,
Her favourite blossom she once said,
I drove away within the hour,
Her words still ringing in my head.

I hadn't planned to leave so soon,
It seemed I'd lost my way in life,
I got back home that afternoon,
My heart felt pierced – as by a knife.

But time permits such wounds to heal,
Forgetting words that once were said,
As months pass by, the less you feel
When other passions rule your head.

Now every year when spring returns,
The cherry trees are out once more,
Reminding me – my heart still yearns
For love I had in Appledore.

Part 8

Free Verse and Imitation

Paranoia

I venture down the street, hurrying,
People are everywhere, walking,
Stopping, standing, waiting,
Faces turn towards me, watching,
Gazing, gaping, staring,
Eyes locked on me, scrutinising,
Probing, penetrating, piercing,
Stabbing deep into my soul,
Leaving me oozing, ebbing.

I dart into a supermarket, hiding,
People are everywhere, bustling,
Choosing, buying, taking,
They're in my way, blocking,
Frowning, scowling, glaring,
Hands seem to clutch at me, grasping,
Grabbing, pulling, pushing,
Sapping the strength from my body,
Leaving me weakening, waning.

I rush out of the supermarket, sweating,
People are everywhere, talking,
Chattering, nattering, gossiping,
Voices circle round me, muttering,
Scoffing, sniggering, sneering,
My mind is awash with noise, swirling,
Laughing, mocking, jeering,
Spinning in a maelstrom of scorn,
Leaving me sinking, drowning.

Feeding the Squirrels

They are coming, I hear them,
The Tall Ones, I see them now,
They are not quiet like our kind,
They cannot move gracefully on the ground,
Nor do they even climb.

They are closer now,
I will let them see me.
"Tall Ones! Can you not see me?
Have you no eyes, Tall Ones?"
The Great Flying One will be watching,
They are not aware or alert.
One has seen me, they are stopping.

Look how they are dropping their food!
They are so wasteful,
I will eat all I can
Then I will hide some food,
For I am quick and clever.

"Tall Ones! If you lose your food
You will have nothing to eat!
You will become still and cold;
The Great Flying One will come,
It will rip you with its hooked beak."
I know the Great Flying One watches me,
It would like to catch me in its claws.
"I am not still and cold, Flying One!
You cannot catch me!"

The Tall Ones are very near me now,
They have no tails, they move awkwardly.
One is trying to get closer – I will not allow it.
"Watch how gracefully I move, Tall One!
Look how my red coat shines in the light,
See my handsome tail!"

Now the Tall Ones are going away,
They always drop their food,
I will eat all I can,
Then I will hide some food,
For I am quick and clever.

Message from Earth

'Calling occupants of interplanetary craft!'
This is the Earth. Go away!
We don't wish to meet you!
'Planet Earth is blue
And there's nothing here for you!'
We don't want your beaming diplomats
Beaming down onto earth
And we really don't need some alien geek
Telling us how to run our world.
If your home planet is so great,
Why are you light years away from it?
You wouldn't like us, anyway!

Don't fly over our land
Because our Air Force will be after you!
And if you fly over our seas
'Bang, bang, our Navy's shot you down!'
We told you that you wouldn't like us!

Don't come here telling us
That you've been sent from God,
You'll probably get crucified.
It's an old tradition here on Earth
And if we don't like your religious views
You'll very likely be burnt at the stake!
That's the way we do things here.

'Hey there! You with the stars in your eyes,'
We have no need for your clever ideas
And your theories about the universe,
We are quite happy here
Doing our Sudoku puzzles.

We do not want you on Earth,
Trampling in our lovely meadows
With your gruesome three-toed feet!
And don't send us images
Of your favourite alien offspring,
With its single snail like eye,
Because – guess what!
'Return to sender.'

We wish to be left alone,
We don't want scaly reptiles
Sat next to us on trains.
We'll only skin you for shoes and handbags
And extract your teeth for necklaces,
It's an old tradition here on earth.
'See you later, alligator!'

'Calling occupants of interplanetary craft!'
This is the Earth – go away!
'Blue, blue, our world is blue,
We're fully booked, no room for you!'
Come back 'in the year 2525'.
Have you tried next door?
Venus has vacancies
And Mercury is really hot stuff.
'Warp on by,' lizard guy!
'*Arrivaderci*...roamer!'

Underwater

The water is cold, it chills my blood,
I must be strong and hold my nerve.
The cold creeps swiftly up over my body
Until only my head is above the surface;
I try hard to control the alarm
That is growing inside me.
I close my eyes as my face is immersed,
Then water enters my nostrils
And I completely lose control;
Panic utterly overwhelms me,
I'm going under, entirely under.
I struggle to get back to the air
But I'm prevented from reaching it,
Unable to regain the surface,
Knowing it's so close
But being held under,
Submerged and drowning,
My worst nightmare!

I am desperate to inhale
And cannot hold my breath any longer,
I must fight, fight for my life!
One final attempt to break through,
My lungs are bursting – this is it!
With all the strength I have left,
I thrust my body upwards
To the life that waits above,
Flailing in a frenzy of terror,
Inches seeming like miles,
Seconds seeming like hours.

At last, my head breaks the surface
And only just in time,
I gulp in the sweet air
That I so desperately need.
A fog envelops my mind,
And stars dance before my eyes,
As I greedily inhale huge volumes
Of the life giving atmosphere.

Slowly, I drag myself out of the water
And with weakened legs
Scramble onto the bank,
Coughing and gasping,
Sick to my stomach, completely spent.
I flop face down on the ground
And kiss the wonderful earth
To which I belong,
My emotions too strong for me to resist.

"Are you all right?" they ask me.
I should never have agreed to be baptised!

Mission to Mars

Behold, I am the fourth
of nine sister worlds,
orbiting a mother star.
For billions of my years
I have been circling
with my two silent moons,
anticipating my destiny,
barren, cold, lifeless,
waiting, waiting.

Everywhere I am desert,
red dust and boulders.
Nowhere is the life
for which I was intended.
I have no purpose
as I circle my star
endlessly, eternally.
waiting, waiting.

My crust no longer
shakes and trembles
from the forces within.
No longer does it hold
lakes of life giving water.
No longer does it embrace
warmth from my mother star,
as I circle around,
barren, cold, lifeless,
waiting, waiting.

But now, what is this?
Something new and exciting
exists on my surface,
in the heart of my barren
dry, dusty deserts.
Something strange
not of my making,
not of my nature,
something alien,
a life thing, a life form
has somehow arrived.

I could destroy it
with my powerful storms,
envelop it, smother it
with my red sands.
But I shall not,
for now I am needed,
I have a purpose,
a reason to exist.
This life form can prosper,
then my waiting will end,
my destiny will be fulfilled.

Daddy-Long-Legs

I saw it at the window
of my spare room,
the daddy-long-legs
scrabbling for a hold on the glass,
desperately trying to get out.
Impressed by its struggles
I resolved to return
and free the poor creature.
I'll be back – I promised
not in the way
of a time travelling terminator,
more in the spirit
of a Buddhist monk.

Too late the next day
I remembered my promise
and found the daddy-long-legs
bereft of any dancing movement,
lifeless on the windowsill.
What have I done – I thought,
my conscience troubling me.
Perhaps this was a champion
amongst daddy-long-legs.
Perhaps the last of a line
of royal ancestry.
Perhaps it was the Albert Einstein
of the insect world.
Who knows? I certainly didn't.

Later, it occurred to me
that maybe, one day
I'll be trapped in my house
in a spreading fire,
scrabbling at the window
desperately trying to get out.
And God, sympathetically looks on.
I'll be back – he promises
as he rushes off to get help.
But then he's distracted
by a persistently annoying
daddy-long-legs,
so fails to return in time
and his conscience troubles him.

So next time you see
a daddy-long-legs
dancing your window pane,
allow it to escape.
Because in the next life,
as Buddhist monks believe,
you may be reincarnated,
not in the image of God,
but as a crane-fly!
Who knows? I certainly don't!

Sanctuary

Just a normal Saturday afternoon,
window shopping, relaxing
mingling with the crowds,
in the new shopping mall.
So civilized, these new malls,
sheltered from the weather,
so safe, these new malls,
separated from the traffic,
so pleasant, these new malls
with light music playing.

Then suddenly the music dying,
a voice booming over the loudspeakers,
catching me unawares,
interrupting my thoughts,
advising us all to leave.
A bomb warning!

Stopping in my tracks
I'm trying to make sense
of the unwelcome message.
It must be a false alarm,
some idiot's idea of a joke.
But this was the 1980's,
time of the IRA campaign
– it might be for real!
How could it be happening
in this safe, civilized centre
with its light music playing?

Then suddenly feeling vulnerable,
enclosed all around,
trapped in a place ideal for a bomb,
maximum carnage,
and I'm the cannon fodder.
Instinctively, I'm joining others
heading for the exit,
only one thought in mind
getting out of this place!
Out in the street, where it's safer.

With more shoppers joining,
the fleeing few became a flow,
no panic, just concern.
People trickling out of coffee bars,
joining the flow
like streams feeding a river.
Shoppers pouring out
of a department store,
uncertain, changing direction
like eddies in a current.
The voice booming out again,
repeating its message,
increasing the pace of the crowd
as concern grows into anxiety.
Children struggling to keep up,
aware of the tension, starting to cry.

Continued

At last, reaching the exit,
stepping outside with relief,
crossing the road
wandering down a side street,
distancing myself
from the danger zone.
As if in a dream,
I'm entering a park in sunshine,
strolling past flowering shrubs,
watching children playing,
people feeding the ducks.

It was like stepping
into another world,
another dimension,
a sanctuary, where people
were blissfully unaware
of events nearby.
So safe, peaceful and civilized,
detached from that other world,
that other dimension,
of the shopping mall,
the anxious crowds
and bomb warnings.

The Last Tigers *(with apologies to William Blake)*

Tiger, tiger, fear your plight,
In the forests few in sight,
Not immortal, doomed to die
And in our hearts the guilt will lie.

What dread weapon, what dread aim
Could quench the brightness of your flame?
And when your heart just fails to beat,
Our dread eyes that yours will meet.

When the fire of your great eyes
Flickers low and slowly dies,
Will we smile our work to see,
Will we who slay the lamb, slay thee?

What the logic, what the brain,
Can be joyful when you're slain,
What the forest, what the moor,
Forever silent from your roar.

When our children reap their fears
And water forests with their tears,
Will we falter, will we sigh,
When our children ask us…why?

Tiger, tiger, roar and bite,
For the forests you must fight,
For a future wild and free,
A feline king for all to see.

Notes

Ingleborough and Whernside are two of the famous "Three Peaks" of Yorkshire, England, which together with the third peak, Pen-y-ghent, make up a challenging circular walk that all serious walkers in England aspire to complete. Twistleton Fell, otherwise known as Scales Moor, is on the west end of the Whernside ridge. The author has spent many hours exploring the wonderful limestone scenery in these areas.

The poem "Secrets near Silverdale" refers to the village of Silverdale, near Carnforth in Lancashire, England. The poem is of course a puzzle, with helpful cryptic clues and all those who are knowledgeable about that area should be able to work out the answers. Visitors can enjoy exploring the regions associated with the poem and try to figure out the answers for themselves.

"Poetry of the Planets" – new facts are being discovered about the planets of the solar system almost every year – with many surprises. This poem will therefore probably occasionally need updating by the author.

"The Mad Boffins' Tea Party" – of course, this poem is a fantasy. The author would be doing Einstein, Newton and the others an injustice if he was seriously suggesting that they didn't understand the tidal effect of the moon (and the sun).

"The Last Tigers" – the author hopes that William Blake would forgive him for manipulating his poetry in this way, especially if it helps to draw attention to the plight of the tiger.

The tiger is the most admired and respected and the most beautiful large predator in the animal kingdom, so surely it's worth the effort and expense to save this animal from extinction.

Acknowledgments

The author would like to thank members of the local Fylde poetry and writing groups, especially Victoria Copeland, whose constructive criticism and encouragement have been so beneficial to his work.

The author would also like to thank the NASA agency, for its excellent space photographs in the public domain, which inspired the ideas for the artistic impressions illustrating two of the poems ("A Shining Light" and "Jewel of the Night"). These illustrations are artistic interpretations and not claimed to be accurate portrayals of space images.